LEAVING A

GODLY LEGACY

BY

CHARLES F. STANLEY

THOMAS NELSON
Since 1798

NASHVILLE   DALLAS   MEXICO CITY   RIO DE JANEIRO

Leaving a Godly Legacy

Charles F. Stanley

Copyright © 1999, 2008 by Charles F. Stanley

Published in Nashville, Tennessee, by Thomas Nelson, Inc.

Editing, layout, and design by Gregory C. Benoit Publishing, Old Mystic, CT

ISBN 978-1-4185-2818-8

Printed in the United States of America

09 10 11 WC 8 7 6 5 4 3

Contents

Placing Priority on a Spiritual Legacy

The Bible is the most practical, down-to-earth book on parenting that has ever been written. It covers every area of raising godly children, including what it means to leave a godly legacy. Yet people wonder whether the Bible is for *this* generation, and they wonder about their own capacity to be a good parent.

Let me assure you that the Bible is for today. No situation that your family encounters is different *in nature* from the situations encountered by families in biblical times. The human heart has not changed. Parents and children still face the same challenges that parents and children faced thousands of years ago.

Let me also assure you that you *can* be a godly parent and leave a good spiritual and emotional legacy to your children, regardless of what may have happened to you as a child. God desires to free you from the bad teaching that you may have received and to heal you of hurts that you may have experienced as a child. You do not need to imitate your own parents—you can imitate your heavenly Father in your child-rearing.

As you study God's principles for a godly legacy, I encourage you to go to your Bible and underline phrases, highlight words or verses, and make notes in the margins to record the specific ways that God speaks to you as a parent. I believe in a well-marked Bible.

This book can be used by you alone or by several people in a small-group study. At various times, you will be asked to relate to the material in one of these four ways:

1. What new insights have you gained? Make notes about the insights that you have. You may want to record them in your Bible or in a separate journal. As you reflect back over your insights, you are likely to see how God has moved in your life.

2. Have you ever had a similar experience? Each of us approaches the Bible from a unique background—our own particular set of relationships and experiences. Our experiences do not make the Bible true—the Word of God is truth regardless of our opinion about it. It is important, however, to share our experiences in order to see how God's truth can be applied to human lives.

3. How do you feel about the material presented? Emotional responses do not give validity to the Scriptures, nor should we trust our emotions as a gauge for our faith. In small-group Bible study, however, it is good for participants to express their emotions. The Holy Spirit often communicates with us through this unspoken language.

4. In what way do you feel challenged to respond or to act? God's Word may cause you to feel inspired or challenged to change something in your life. Take the challenge seriously and find ways of acting upon it. If God reveals to you a particular need that He wants *you* to address, take that as "marching orders" from God. God is expecting you to *do* something with the challenge that He has just given you.

Start and conclude your Bible study sessions in prayer. Ask God to give you spiritual eyes to see and spiritual ears to hear. As you conclude your study, ask the Lord to seal what you have learned so that you will never forget it. Ask Him to help you grow into the fullness of the stature of Christ Jesus.

I caution you to keep the Bible at the center of your study. A genuine Bible study stays focused on God's Word and promotes a growing faith and a closer walk with the Holy Spirit in *each* person who participates.

2

The Inheritance That Really Matters

❧ In This Lesson ❧

Learning: What exactly *is* a godly legacy?

Growing: How can I influence the next generation for Christ?

When most of us think about leaving or receiving an "inheritance," we automatically think in terms of money and property, including personal items of sentimental value. But the Bible presents a much more important legacy that we as Christian parents and grandparents are to leave to our children. It is the legacy that lies in the emotional and spiritual realms—a legacy of lifelong benefit and eternal value.

Much of what we know about leaving a godly legacy can be found in the writings of Paul. He spells out in clear terms how Christians are to express their belief in Christ Jesus and how Christians are to treat one another. Paul uses two phrases that deserve our attention at the outset of our discussion.

❧ When you hear the word *legacy*, what comes to your mind?

3

✍. What type of emotional legacy do you desire to leave the next generation? What type of spiritual legacy do you desire to leave the children in your life?

Live a life worthy of our calling

The word *worthy* may also be translated as "weighty." Paul called upon Christians to leave a weighty imprint wherever they walked. Imagine for a moment that a person is walking through a slab of wet concrete. The heavier the person, the deeper and more distinct the footprints. As believers in Christ Jesus, we are not to wander aimlessly through life or to have futile thinking. We are to walk with purpose, intending to leave a deep imprint on the lives of all we touch—and especially so on our children. This imprint is to be "weighty" and lasting—we are to leave a permanent imprint upon our children.

Finally, this weighty imprint is to be one that is directly related to our calling. The word *calling* does not refer to a full-time ministry or to a specific call of God to undertake a particular project. Our calling is to be Christlike. As Paul wrote in Philippians 3:14, "I press toward the goal for the prize of the upward call of God in Christ Jesus." Our calling is to a higher morality, a higher ethical standard, a higher spiritual plane, a higher way of living—one that culminates in our walking in righteousness every day of our lives and then walking into our perfection in heaven. We are to leave a weighty, permanent imprint of God's love, goodness, and forgiveness wherever we walk, for as long as we walk on this earth.

☙ What is "the upward call of God" that Paul refers to?

☙ What goals are you presently striving toward? How will your striving for that goal influence your children?

Imitators of Christ

Paul states in Ephesians 5:1, "Be imitators of God ... as dearly loved children" (NIV). The legacy that we leave to our children is to be one of Christlikeness. To be an imitator of Christ is to mimic Christ, to mirror Him, to copy Him. To be a follower of Christ Jesus means that we are to develop the same character that Christ Jesus displayed, relate to other people as Christ Jesus related to them, and to obey God the Father as Christ Jesus obeyed Him. We are to love sacrificially and to pour out our lives in service to others. In every aspect of our attitude, conversation, and behavior, we are to imitate Christ to our children.

5

⮑ When have you seen children imitating your behavior? How did you feel?

⮑ What aspect of Christ's life have you consciously tried to imitate?

How Children Learn

Paul stated a very important concept regarding imitating Christ: we are to be "as dear children." Paul knew that children learn first by copying the behavior of their parents. We have all seen a little child who walks just like his daddy or tosses her head just like her mother. Children learn best by imitating others. They learn to talk, walk, handle objects, and behave toward other people as they see their parents talking, walking, handling objects, and behaving toward others.

A baby has the potential to learn any language—but the language which your child learns is the language that you speak, including your inflections, accent, and vocabulary. A baby has the potential to walk—but when and how that baby walks is directly related to the way the parents demonstrate how to walk. A newborn baby has the potential to learn to use chopsticks or a fork—whichever you use, your child will learn to use. And the same is true for everything from tying shoelaces to using a toothbrush.

The way that you treat other people is going to be the way that your child treats them. The attitudes that you have are going to be the first attitudes that your child has. The nature of your conversation is going to become the nature of your child's conversation.

What an awesome responsibility a parent has to be an "imitator of Christ" because, as the parent imitates Christ, the child is going to imitate the parent. This is the way that children "learn Christ." They learn how to be a Christian and what it means to accept Christ, follow Christ, and develop a personal relationship with Christ first and foremost from their parents.

∝ In what areas do you struggle the most as a parent?

Never Forgotten

A material or financial legacy can be squandered or misused. An emotional and spiritual legacy may be ignored or rebelled against by a child, but it can never be forgotten. The way that you live becomes a legacy that will always be with your child—for better or worse. What you do will always be more powerful than what you say. For a legacy to

7

have maximum impact, beliefs must line up with words, which in turn must line up with deeds. There must be a consistency of Christlikeness throughout a parent's life if the spiritual legacy is going to be of greatest value.

The question naturally arises, "What things are most important for me to leave my children as an emotional and spiritual legacy?" This question is at the heart of this Bible study. We will take a look at what I believe to be the foundation stones of a godly legacy. A child who receives the emotional and spiritual legacy identified in this book is going to have all that is necessary for living a moral, Christ-centered, wise, loving, and eternal life.

Spiritual Children, Too

You may not be a parent or grandparent. You may be an aunt or uncle, a teacher or someone who works regularly with children. You may simply be a Christian adult in the body of Christ. This book is for you, too!

Each of us is called to leave a godly legacy to all who see our lives, and that includes the lives of children that we may not even know. It also includes the lives of those who are our "spiritual children"—the children of all ages whom we lead to Christ and help nurture and raise up to maturity in Christ. The legacy that you leave to your spiritual children is no less important than the legacy left by parents to their natural-born children.

Ask God today to help you identify children in your life to whom you can leave a godly legacy. Keep these children in mind as you do this study. They will make it even more personal and meaningful to you.

Identify some of your fears as a parent—and also some of your hopes and joys.

What aspects of your life would you most like your children to imitate? What aspects would you *least* like them to imitate?

Today and Tomorrow

TODAY: CHILDREN LEARN BEST BY IMITATING—AND THEY ARE IMITATING ME.

TOMORROW: I WILL BEGIN TO CONSCIOUSLY IMITATE JESUS CHRIST THIS WEEK.

LESSON 2

A Strong Sense of Belonging

---——— &. **In This Lesson** &? ———---

LEARNING: WHAT IS THE MOST IMPORTANT LEGACY THAT I CAN GIVE MY
CHILDREN?

GROWING: HOW CAN I HELP MY CHILDREN FEEL THAT THEY BELONG?

&

One of the greatest gifts that you can give to your child is a strong sense of belonging—both to your family and to the greater family of Christ. Every parent knows that he needs to provide the basics for children—food, shelter, clothing, safety. Equally important, however, is the need to provide the basics for the emotional well-being of a child. Emotional well-being begins with a sense of belonging.

A sense of belonging is the knowledge that a child is *wanted.* It includes feelings of being cared for, of being appreciated for his uniqueness, of being enjoyed for his personality. A child who does not have a sense of belonging grows up feeling rejected and alienated from other people. Often, the tendency of a child who feels rejected is to seek out those who do want him, even joining a gang or cult. At times, a child who feels rejected spends years, even a lifetime, trying to prove that he is desirable.

∽ When have you felt rejected? How did you compensate for those feelings?

We can be absolutely certain that God *wants* us. He created us, He desires us, He longs to be in close relationship with us. He seeks us out. He invites us to spend time with Him. God's purpose in saving us is that we will live forever with Him in heaven.

Those who leave a godly legacy never exclude other believers—regardless of their denomination—but are quick to express their appreciation for other believers. Paul wrote in Romans 1:11–12, "I long to see you, that I may impart to you some spiritual gift, so that you may be established—that is, that I may be encouraged together with you by the mutual faith both of you and me." He said in Philippians 1:8, "For God is my witness, how greatly I long for you all with the affection of Jesus Christ." Later in his letter, Paul called the Philippians his "beloved and longed-for brethren" (Philippians 4:1). How good the believers in Rome and Philippi must have felt when they read these words!

∽ How does it feel to hear someone say, "I can hardly wait to be with you"?

➳ According to Romans 1:11-12 (above), why does Paul long to see his fellow Christians?

Creating a Sense of Belonging in Your Child

There are two main ways to build a sense of belonging in your child: spend time with your child, and ask him for his ideas and opinions.

1. Give Your Child Time

Children need to spend time with their parents. They need to know that Mom and Dad are always available to them, even if it is by phone. From time to time, every child needs to spend time exclusively with his Mom and Dad. Children need "quality" time, but they also need vast quantities of time.

Never exclude your child from your presence without giving him a specific reason why you need to be alone, and a specific time when you will again be available. Recognize that young children have short attention spans. Take the few seconds required to give your child the hug that he needs, to answer the question that he has, or to show appreciation to your child when he comes seeking your approval.

Jesus is our role model when it comes to taking time to be with children. In Jesus' day, little children were not highly regarded—many adults thought them unworthy of being included in religious gatherings until they were "of age." Jesus did not take that approach. We read in Matthew 19:13–14:

> Then little children were brought to Him that He might put His hands on them and pray, but the disciples rebuked them. But Jesus said, "Let the little children come to Me, and do not forbid them; for of such is the kingdom of heaven."

God's plan for teaching children was that children would be with their parents throughout a day, learning from their parents' example and from frequent, spur-of-the-moment conversations as various situations arose. We read this in Deuteronomy 6:6–7:

> These words which I command you today shall be in your heart; you shall teach them diligently to your children, and shall talk of them when you sit in your house, when you walk by the way, when you lie down, and when you rise up.

God expected children to learn about His commandments and His great love through *being with their parents*—by hearing their parents speak of obedience to a loving God, and by watching their parents as they serve God. When we spend time with our children, we teach them that God, their heavenly Father, always has time for them. He is always available to them, always desires to be with them, and always longs to be in an intimate, loving relationship with them.

And Jesus, perceiving the thought of their heart, took a little child and set him by Him, and said to them, "Whoever receives this little child in My name receives Me; and whoever receives Me receives Him who sent Me. For he who is least among you all will be great."

—Luke 9:47-48

What does it mean to "receive" a child in Jesus' name? How is this done in practical terms?

What do these verses imply about a person who does *not* receive a little child in Jesus' name?

2. Value your child's ideas and opinions.

A child feels included if his ideas and opinions are valued and sought out. On the other hand, if parents make all of the decisions and come up with all of the ideas, a child begins to regard his presence as unwanted or unnecessary.

It is also vital that you give validity and importance to your child's questions. When you take time to answer your child's questions, you send the message, "I want you to know what I know. I want to share a mutual life with you." The Lord is never too tired or too busy to hear from us—to hear our petitions, our praises, our questions, our hopes.

> Now it came to pass, as He was praying in a certain place, when He ceased, that one of His disciples said to Him, "Lord, teach us to pray, as John also taught his disciples." So He said to them....
>
> —Luke 11:1-2

 Note that Jesus was busy praying when He was interrupted. How did He respond? What did His response demonstrate to the disciples?

 How do you respond when your children interrupt important tasks? What does your response teach your children?

The Great Value that God Places on "Belonging"

Throughout the New Testament, we find great value placed on "belonging"—both to God and to the family of God. John stated in his Gospel that Jesus came to this earth to show us what the Father is like and to show us that the Father desires to be in relationship with us: "The Word became flesh and dwelt among us, and we beheld His glory" (John 1:14). God wants us to belong to Him, to know Him, to be reconciled to Him.

Jesus was in close fellowship with His disciples. He broke bread with them, He walked with them, He invited them to participate fully in His ministry. His final prayer for them was that they—and we—might become one with Him.

> [Jesus prayed for his disciples:] "And the glory which You gave Me I have given them, that they may be one just as We are one: I in them, and You in Me; that they may be made perfect in one, and that the world may know that You have sent Me, and have loved them as You have loved Me."
>
> —John 17:22-23

☙ What does it mean that Jesus was "one" with the Father? What does this mean regarding the disciples' relationships with one another?

How can your family gain that sort of "oneness"? According to these verses, what is the result of strong family unity?

God's plan was for the church to be a community that lived in unity of Spirit. Every believer was expected to be linked to every other believer in "one body" and "one faith." Jesus taught this clearly in Matthew 18:19–20:

> Again I say to you that if two of you agree on earth concerning anything that they ask, it will be done for them by My Father in heaven. For where two or three are gathered together in My name, I am there in the midst of them.

Every believer should be made to feel at home within the church, and part of the family—no believer should be excluded. When we teach our children that they belong to us and belong to our families as worthy members, we teach them what it means to belong to God. We give them the desire to belong to God. We help them to see themselves as belonging fully in the Body of Christ, and they will one day extend a sense of belonging to other believers, as well. "To belong" is a great and godly legacy which we must give to our children!

That which we have seen and heard we declare to you, that you also may have fellowship with us; and truly our fellowship is with the Father and with His Son Jesus Christ.

—1 John 1:3

What things is John "declaring" to his readers? What things do you "declare" to your children?

How well do your words line up with your actions in front of children? In what areas do you need to be more consistent with the teachings of Christ?

Today and Tomorrow

TODAY: A SENSE OF BELONGING IS VITAL TO A CHILD'S WELL-BEING, AND WILL INFLUENCE HOW HE TREATS OTHERS.

TOMORROW: I WILL MAKE MY CHILDREN A TOP PRIORITY, MORE IMPORTANT THAN OTHER "IMPORTANT" TASKS.

Lesson 3

A Strong Sense of Value

---------------- ❧ **In This Lesson** ❧ ----------------

LEARNING: WHAT IS UNCONDITIONAL LOVE?

GROWING: HOW CAN I LEARN TO LOVE OTHERS—ESPECIALLY MY CHIL-
DREN—WITHOUT STRINGS?

Everybody needs to feel loved—to feel that he has value in another person's eyes. To be loved is to gain self-worth. Unconditional love creates security in a child; conditional love based on "ifs," "whens," and "buts" creates doubt. The earlier that a person experiences unconditional love in his life, the more solid the foundation for his emotional development and well-being.

One of the greatest messages that you can ever convey to your child is this: "I love you solely because you are *you*. I thank God that He created you and put you into my life."

❧ When have you experienced unconditional love? What was the effect?

19

A message of unconditional love also tells a child that he is "lovable"—not only to other people, but to God. The child who experiences unconditional love is far less likely to perceive God as a harsh, punitive judge and far more likely to perceive Him as a loving, giving, merciful Heavenly Father.

~ How do you feel when you think about God? Do you feel openness and love toward God, or do you feel fear or reluctance to approach Him?

One of the greatest gifts that you can ever give to a child is a perception of God as a loving, forgiving Father. Such a perception makes it far more likely that your child is going to desire to communicate with God, grow in his relationship with God, and turn to God in any time of crisis or need.

> And we have known and believed the love that God has for us. God is love, and he who abides in love abides in God, and God in him.
>
> —1 John 4:16

~ How does a person "abide in God"? How does a child do the same with parents?

ᐧᐁ Consider your answer to the earlier question about how you feel when approaching God. How do your children feel when approaching you?

ᢁ Freedom to Love ᢁ

The child who experiences unconditional love is much freer in expressing love to other people. In fact, a person who has not experienced unconditional love has a great deal of difficulty loving others. He has no basis for knowing how to love and is far more likely to be manipulative and controlling when it comes to matters of the heart. Relationships crumble when love is given conditionally with a constant undercurrent of "I'll love you if you ...", or "I love you when you ...", or "I can't love you unless you ...."

Unless a person receives God's unconditional love, he cannot love as God loves. God's loving poured into us and *through us* enables us to accept and to love fully.

ᐧᐁ Do you struggle to love people unconditionally? Do you sometimes put conditions on relationships?

This is My commandment, that you love one another as I have loved you.

—John 15:12

↞ How has God loved you? How does that compare with the way that you love your children?

Three Results of Unconditional Love

Apart from having an ability and freedom to love others, unconditional love produces three things in your child that are of great benefit throughout your child's life: a genuine spontaneity in giving to others, to the point of self-sacrifice; an increased ability to trust God; and a greater desire to keep God's commandments.

1. Sacrificial giving

Genuine love is always sacrificial love. Jesus is certainly our role model in this. He loved to the point of giving His life so that those who believe in Him might receive eternal life. Parents, too, are called to give sacrificially to their children—to put the child's needs above their own needs and to give sacrificially of their time and energy.

This does not mean that a parent should strive to provide all of a child's *wants*. True love means doing what is *best* for a child in all situations, and it is never best to give a child everything that he desires. A child needs to earn some things and to wait for some things. A child should never have to wait or earn, however, an expression of a parent's love: a smile, an encouraging word, a hug, or the spoken words, "I love you."

Sacrificial giving on the part of a parent includes making the effort to attend your child's games or performances, even if you are exhausted; going to church with your child *every Sunday,* even if you'd rather sleep in or play golf; taking time to read to, play with, and pray with your child, even if there is work to get done; taking time to listen to your child, answer questions, and comfort your child, even if it means asking another adult to wait for you.

Paul wrote to the Ephesians that our sacrificial loving—which is loving as Christ loved—produces a "sweet-smelling aroma" before God. In other words, sacrificial love is *pleasing* to God. It is a way of honoring Him and of responding in a right way to His sacrificial love for us. The child who experiences sacrificial love learns by your example what it means to be a giving, unselfish person. Such a person can really be used by God in all types of ministry!

∼ When have you been the recipient of sacrificial giving? How did you feel? What was your response to that kind of love?

Greater love has no one than this, than to lay down one's life
for his friends.

—John 15:13

❧ Give practical examples of what it means to "lay down one's
life". Which of these things have you done for your children?

2. Trust in God

It is much easier to trust people when you know that they love you unconditionally. This includes our ability to trust God: it is much easier to
trust an unconditionally loving heavenly Father to meet our needs, than
to trust a God whom we perceive to be unmerciful, harsh, and critical!

A person who cannot trust others, and who does not trust God, is mis-
erable and feels that he must make things happen, in his own life and
in the lives of others. Such a person often becomes manipulative and
suspicious of the motives of others. At the same time, no person can
control everything, and the untrusting person is likely to experience
increasing disappointment, anxiety, frustration, and depression.

The person who is able to receive God's unconditional love believes,
*God is on my side. He loves me and desires what is good for me. He is
going to act in a way that is eternally beneficial to me. I can trust Him
with this situation, this relationship, and all of my life.*

The child who learns to trust is willing to take risks in sharing his personal testimony about God's love. Such a child is not afraid of criticism and rejection because he knows that the most important thing in life is God's love and forgiveness, and that God will always be present in his life—now and forever. Above all, a child who knows that he is loved unconditionally and eternally by God is freed from the deep inner fear that plagues so many people in our stress-filled world. To be loved by God and to trust God are vital for a person to feel secure.

> There is no fear in love; but perfect love casts out fear, because fear involves torment. But he who fears has not been made perfect in love.
>
> —1 John 4:18

⁓ What sorts of fears have you experienced in love? What fears do you have toward God?

⁓ What might your children fear in their relationship to you? How can you "cast out fear" from their hearts?

3. Keeping God's commandments

A loving parent always sets boundaries for a child—not to punish or to break the spirit of the child, but to keep the child from those things that the parent knows will bring harm. In the same way, our loving heavenly Father has given us His commandments. They are for our eternal *good*.

If a child grows up believing that a parent's love is based upon conditions—including the condition of obedience—that child is going to resent a parent's rules and is very likely going to rebel against them. However, a child is much more likely to obey if he grows up believing that a parent's love is unconditional and that their rules are a by-product of their love.

Part of trusting God is trusting that God's commandments and laws are for our benefit. When we know that God's rules are for our *good*, we are much more likely to keep them! The result of obedience to God, of course, is that we are in a position to receive all that the Lord may desire to give to us. God can trust the obedient person with His greatest blessings.

᠌ᠸ Have you had experience with rebellion in your past? What were the consequences?

Observe and obey all these words which I command you, that it may go well with you and your children after you forever, when you do what is good and right in the sight of the LORD your God.

—Deuteronomy 12:28

🔊 Why does God promise that obedience to His Word makes things "go well" with your children, as well as with you? What areas of God's Word do you need to follow more closely?

Every parent that I know desires that their children grow up to love God, to trust God, and to keep God's commandments. Every parent wants their children to be unselfish, to love and trust others, and to live in right relationships with others. The key to these qualities in a child's life is *unconditional love!*

Unconditional love gives your child a strong sense of worthiness and value. If a child knows that there is no end to the love that is flowing toward him, he will be willing to risk giving his own love away freely.

If a son asks for bread from any father among you, will he give him a stone? Or if he asks for a fish, will he give him a serpent instead of a fish? Or if he asks for an egg, will he offer him a scorpion? If you then, being evil, know how to give good gifts to your children, how much more will your heavenly Father give the Holy Spirit to those who ask Him!

—Luke 11:11-13

How often do you ask God to help you love your children unconditionally?

What help does Jesus promise to those who ask?

Today and Tomorrow

TODAY: GOD LOVES ME UNCONDITIONALLY, AND I MUST LEARN TO IMITATE THAT LOVE FOR OTHERS.

TOMORROW: I WILL ASK THE LORD TO HELP ME, THROUGH HIS HOLY SPIRIT, TO LOVE OTHERS UNCONDITIONALLY.

LESSON 4

An Awareness of Capability

---------------- ❧ **In This Lesson** ☙ ----------------

LEARNING: WHAT SHOULD I BE TRAINING MY CHILD TO DO WHEN HE GROWS UP?

GROWING: HOW CAN I IDENTIFY MY CHILD'S NATURAL ABILITIES?

---------------- ∞ ----------------

One of the greatest gifts that you can give your child is to help him discover and develop unique talents. Every child needs to know that he is capable of doing something that is good, beneficial, or helpful. An awareness of capability is vital for emotional health and well-being.

Awareness of capability is an important foundation for a child to believe that he has something of *eternal* benefit to offer the world. Our capability in Christ Jesus includes spiritual gifts—those that the Holy Spirit imparts to us as permanent ministry gifts, and those that the Holy Spirit imparts to us temporarily as He wills.

A child who has a strong understanding that he can contribute to the family, to society, to the church, and to the kingdom of God has purpose, focus, direction, and a greater desire to develop personal talents with enthusiasm.

❧ What are your own "capabilities"? What are you child's God-given talents?

❧ How does it feel to know that you are good at something and that what you do helps others? How much do you encourage your children's gifts and talents?

Every Child Is Gifted

Every child has been gifted by God. Each person has been given talents and abilities from birth. The challenge for most parents is that a child's God-given gifts may not be the gifts that the *parent* wanted his child to have. We see this in the mother who wants her daughter to become an actress because the mother has always desired to be an actress, or the father who demands that his son become a better athlete than he ever was. Proverbs 22:6 is one of the most quoted and least understood verses in the Bible:

> Train up a child in the way he should go, And when he is old he
> will not depart from it.

Many parents read this verse as "train up a child in the way that I want
my child to go." The truth is that we are to train up our children in the
way that God has designed for them from their birth. Certainly that
means obeying God's commandments, receiving Christ's forgiveness,
and walking in righteousness—but it also means unlocking and developing the unique gifts that God has given to the child. It means developing all of the *child's* God-given abilities, not demanding that the
child pursue all parent-desired opportunities.

Parents must also understand that their spiritual gifts and those of
their child may differ. Many parents want their children to follow in
their particular ministries or spiritual gifts. God may very well have a
different idea. The goal that every parent faces is to help a child discover *his* gifts, both natural and spiritual.

⮶ What does it mean, in practical terms, to "train up a child in
the way that he should go"?

⮶ What ministries might God be planning for your children in
the future? How can you train them now to exercise those gifts
later?

Unique and Wonderful Gifts

Every child should be encouraged by the good news that he has been given unique and wonderful gifts by a loving heavenly Father. God declares that every aspect of creation "is good"! He declares the same about every child born. A child's gifts are *good,* and they are intended to produce good on the earth. Human beings may prize certain gifts more than others, but God gives gifts as *He* wills and, from His perspective, all gifts and talents are good and have the seed of benefit in them.

Furthermore, no two people will function in their gifts in precisely the same way because we each have different personalities, skills, life experiences, and emotional temperaments. Encourage your child to discover his unique gifts and to express his talents in the way that is uniquely his own.

> Behold, I have created the blacksmith Who blows the coals in the fire, Who brings forth an instrument for his work....

> —Isaiah 54:16

❧ Do you give thanks to God for the gifts and talents that He has given you? Or do you sometimes wish that He'd given you different abilities?

❧ What gifts and talents does the world esteem the highest? Lowest? What does this verse suggest about that attitude?

Three Key Principles Regarding Your Child's Gifts

There are three key principles regarding your child's giftedness:

    ∽ We must discover and develop God's gifts.

    ∽ God commands us to use our gifts as a means of serving Him and building up the Body of Christ.

    ∽ God wants us to use our gifts in love, with humility, and in peace.

1. We must discover and develop them God's gifts.

No person is given a full-blown gift. Every gift is given to us in the form of "potential." It is up to us to develop our gifts. We do that in cooperation and in relationship with others. The development of gifts begins with an act of faith that the Lord Jesus will help us to become "doers" of the gifts that He has put within us. We only can develop our gifts to a certain degree in our own strength. None of us has the ability within ourselves to *cause* our gifts to bless others or to be of eternal value. It is only as God infuses our gifts with *His* life that they take on eternal benefit and truly become life-giving.

Our challenge is to ask God to help us in developing our gifts: to give us wise and skilled teachers; to help us develop our gifts with patience, discipline, and diligence; and to give us courage to use our gifts in relationship with other people. You can always assure your child of one thing: no matter what gift may be given to your child, God will help him develop that gift and use it in a way that will bring glory to God's name. Every gift can become an effective tool for ministry and for soul-winning under the guidance of the Holy Spirit.

Therefore I remind you to stir up the gift of God which is in you....

—2 Timothy 1:6

≈ What does it mean, in practical terms, to "stir up the gift of God which is in you"?

≈ What are you doing to "stir up" the gifts that God has given you? To stir up your children's gifts?

2. God commands us to use our gifts as a means of serving Him and building up the Body of Christ.

The very reason that we are given gifts and talents from God is so that we might use them to benefit others. Believers in Christ are not required to make animal sacrifices as the Israelites did in the Old Testament, but we *are* called to present our own lives—our talents, time, energy, gifts—as a form of "living sacrifice" to the Lord. The Lord doesn't want only a part of us—He desires all of us to be yielded to Him and available for service to others as He inspires us to act, to speak, and to give.

> You did not choose Me, but I chose you and appointed you that you should go and bear fruit, and that your fruit should remain, that whatever you ask the Father in My name He may give you.
>
> —John 15:16

What does it mean to "go and bear fruit"? What does it mean "that your fruit should remain"?

What things can you do this week to help your children to "go and bear fruit"?

3. God wants us to use our gifts in love, with humility, and in peace.

Only Jesus embodied all spiritual gifts, but each of us has been given the privilege of expressing one facet of the Lord's ministry. Regardless of the gifts we have been given, we are to manifest the *character* of Christ: love, joy, peace, longsuffering, kindness, goodness, faithfulness, gentleness, and self-control (Galatians 5:22–23). Regardless of the gifts that we have been given, we are to offer them freely and with humility to other believers.

God has no tolerance for pride. A natural talent or spiritual gift should never be regarded as a cause for pride. Our gifts come from God, are developed as God allows us to develop them, and are of use and eternal benefit only as God provides *His* opportunities and blessing. All glory, praise, and honor that come from the exercise of our talents should be directed to the Lord! Our praise song should be the same as that of the heavenly host:

Blessing and glory and wisdom,
Thanksgiving and honor and power and might,
Be to our God forever and ever.
Amen.

—Revelation 7:12

Abide in Me, and I in you. As the branch cannot bear fruit of itself, unless it abides in the vine, neither can you, unless you abide in Me. I am the vine, you are the branches. He who abides in Me, and I in him, bears much fruit; for without Me you can do nothing.

—John 15:4-5

∽ What does it mean to "abide" in Christ? Give practical examples of how this is done.

∽ Do you tend to rely on your own abilities, or to ask God regularly for help and guidance? What are you teaching your children in this regard?

One of the greatest things that parents can do for their children is to help them discover their aptitudes and provide lessons and mentors to help them develop their talents. Encourage your child to be diligent in practice. Provide plenty of appreciation and recognition for the talent that your child is developing and the progress that he is making. Recognize that your child is not going to become an expert immediately in the use of his talents. Be patient and encourage a steady growth of capabilities.

Also, keep your own expectations in line as to just how good your child may become in a particular area of talent. Some talents are to be developed solely to give the child joy at being able to participate in a group, or as a means of personally giving praise to God. Some talents may be of great blessing and benefit to other people. Recognize the difference and help your child to differentiate among his own talents and to discern where the greatest focus of time and energy should be placed.

> The hand of the diligent will rule, But the lazy man will be put to forced labor.

> —Proverbs 12:24

What things have you been diligent in developing in your own life? What areas do you tend to be more lazy in?

❧ How can you train your children to be diligent—without being over-bearing or nagging?

> Whatever your hand finds to do, do it with your might; for there is no work or device or knowledge or wisdom in the grave where you are going.
>
> —Ecclesiastes 9:10

❧ What is Solomon's reason for urging us to be diligent in our work? What does death have to do with developing gifts and talents?

❧ Why does Solomon combine "knowledge" and "wisdom" with works of the hands ("work or device")? What part does wisdom play in developing our gifts and talents?

❧ Today and Tomorrow ☙

TODAY: GOD HAS GIVEN GIFTS TO ME AND MY CHILDREN, AND HE WANTS US TO USE THEM TO SERVE OTHERS.

TOMORROW: I WILL ASK THE LORD TO HELP ME DISCERN THE GIFTS AND TALENTS THAT HE HAS GIVEN MY CHILDREN.

Notes and Prayer Requests:

LESSON 5

An Ability to Walk in the Spirit

❧ In This Lesson ❧

LEARNING: WHAT DOES IT MEAN TO "WALK IN THE SPIRIT"?

GROWING: HOW CAN I LEAD MY CHILDREN TO SALVATION?

Every Christian parent's greatest desire is to see his child grow up to love God and to walk daily in the Holy Spirit. As we have covered in previous lessons, the child who receives unconditional love has a strong sense of belonging to family and to the church, and the child who knows that he has been gifted by God develops a *predisposition* to accept God's forgiveness of sin and receive Jesus into his life.

The predisposition to accept Christ and walk in the Spirit does not mean that a child *has* accepted Christ. No parent can receive Christ on behalf of a child. That is a decision that the child must make by exercising his own will. Parents face three challenges in teaching a child to walk in the Spirit:

1. to lead a child to *personally* accept Jesus as his Savior

2. to learn to say no to temptation

3. to learn how to submit to the authority of the Holy Spirit on a daily basis

Leading Your Child to Christ

Your child will imitate you. The more you express *your* dependence upon Jesus Christ as Savior, the more your child will want to call Him Savior. Let your child hear you thank the Lord for forgiving you, cleansing you of your sin nature, and changing your heart so that you have a desire to obey Him. Share your testimony with your child about how *you* accepted Jesus Christ as your Savior. Your child will not think less of you for admitting that you once were a sinner.

The apostle Paul was quick to tell others what Jesus Christ had done in his life. As you read the passage below, note that Paul does not attempt to justify his former life or to make any claim that he deserved to be saved on his own merits:

> I myself thought I must do many things contrary to the name of Jesus of Nazareth. This I also did in Jerusalem, and many of the saints I shut up in prison, having received authority from the chief priests; and when they were put to death, I cast my vote against them. And I punished them often in every synagogue and compelled them to blaspheme; and being exceedingly enraged against them, I persecuted them even to foreign cities.

> While thus occupied, as I journeyed to Damascus with authority and commission from the chief priests, at midday, O king, along the road I saw a light from heaven, brighter than the sun, shining around me and those who journeyed with me. And when we all had fallen to the ground, I heard a voice speaking to me and saying in the Hebrew language, "Saul, Saul, why are you persecuting Me? It is hard for you to kick against the goads." So I said, 'Who are You, Lord?" And He said, "I am Jesus, whom you are persecuting. But rise and stand on your feet; for I have appeared to you for this purpose, to make you a

42

minister and a witness both of the things which you have seen and of the things which I will yet reveal to you. I will deliver you from the Jewish people, as well as from the Gentiles, to whom I now send you, to open their eyes, in order to turn them from darkness to light, and from the power of Satan to God, that they may receive forgiveness of sins and an inheritance among those who are sanctified by faith in Me."

Therefore, King Agrippa, I was not disobedient to the heavenly vision.

—Acts 26:9–19

☙ When and how did you accept Jesus as your Savior? Write down the story below, or in a journal—then share that story with your children this week.

A second thing that a parent must do is to make certain that a child knows that he must accept Jesus for himself—and that he knows how to do so. Assure your child that, when he acknowledges to God that he is a sinner, God is quick to forgive.

> If we confess our sins, He is faithful and just to forgive us our sins and to cleanse us from all unrighteousness.
>
> —1 John 1:9

☙ According to this verse, what must we do to receive salvation?

☙ What is the difference between being forgiven for sins and being cleansed "from all unrighteousness"?

44

A third thing that parents can do to lead a child to Christ is to make sure that the child hears the salvation message often and has ample opportunity to respond to it. Bring your child with you to church every Sunday, and make sure that the church preaches the message of salvation and gives an opportunity for a person to respond to the gospel and accept Christ. Get your child involved in an active Christian youth group and make it possible for him to go on retreats and to camps where the salvation message is preached as part of the overall program.

At the same time, do not allow your child to become involved in activities or relationships in which Jesus is ridiculed, denounced, or rejected as the Son of God. Paul made it clear that, in the "flesh," we respond to various teachings by saying "yes," "no," or "maybe." There are churches who also preach with these various attitudes about Christ—some preach "yes," He is the Son of God and the Savior or mankind; others preach "no," He isn't; and some preach "maybe" He is the Son of God, along with other options. Paul had this to say in 2 Corinthians 1:17–20:

> The things I plan, do I plan according to the flesh, that with me there should be Yes, Yes and No, No? But as God is faithful, our word to you was not Yes and No. For the Son of God, Jesus Christ, who was preached among you by us—by me, Silvanus, and Timothy—was not Yes and No, but in Him was Yes. For all the promises of God in Him are Yes, and in Him Amen, to the glory of God through us.

Your responsibility as a Christian parent is *not* to give your child options about what may or may not be true, but to champion the truth about Jesus Christ as Savior. Protect your child from those influences that lead away from the gospel.

Jesus said to him, "I am the way, the truth, and the life. No one comes to the Father except through Me."

—John 14:6

❧ The world today teaches that there are many paths to God. What does Jesus say about that?

❧ Put into your own words these claims of Jesus:

The way:

The truth:

The life:

Saying No to Temptation

The way that your child learns to say no to temptation is to see *you* say no to temptation. In order for us to choose good and refuse evil, we must first know what *is* good, true, and right before God. Satan presents many counterfeits to the believer and the unbeliever, and it is only as we know the truth that we are able to discern error.

Admit to your child that you struggle with temptation—and that it is not a sin to be tempted. All people are tempted—Jesus Christ Himself was tempted by Satan! Sin occurs when we *give in* to temptation. Help your child to recognize that temptation comes from the enemy of his soul and that the best way to defeat the enemy is the same way that Jesus defeated Satan when He was tempted: by quoting the Word of God. Help your child memorize key verses to use when tempted.

And finally, assure your child that, anytime he resists the devil's temptations, he can overcome the devil and become stronger as a result. Teach your child to pray when he is faced with a temptation: "Lord Jesus, deliver me from evil. Help me to have the courage to stand for what is right." Pray that prayer *with* your child and *for* your child on a regular basis: "Lord Jesus, deliver my child from evil. Help him to have courage to stand up for what is right in every circumstance that he faces today."

Therefore submit to God. Resist the devil and he will flee from you. Draw near to God and He will draw near to you. Cleanse your hands, you sinners; and purify your hearts, you double-minded.

—James 4:7-8

47

‍☙ How does a person do each of the following:

Submit to God:

Resist the devil:

Draw near to God:

Cleanse your hands:

Purify your hearts:

Walking in the Spirit

Paul wrote in Ephesians 5:8–11, 17:

> Walk as children of light (for the fruit of the Spirit is in all goodness, righteousness, and truth), proving what is acceptable to the Lord. And have no fellowship with the unfruitful works of darkness, but rather expose them ... Therefore do not be unwise, but understand what the will of the Lord is.

Walking in the Spirit is a daily process. It is trusting and relying upon the Holy Spirit every day for guidance and courage. Each of us must choose daily to be "filled" with God's Spirit so that everything we say and do is a genuine reflection of Christ Jesus.

Now, we need to make certain that there is no confusion about the "residence" of the Holy Spirit in us. The Holy Spirit indwells every believer at the moment that he receives Jesus Christ as Savior. The Holy Spirit sets up permanent residence in the believer, and He does not depart. We may feel His presence more strongly in us at some times more than other times, but the Holy Spirit does not "leave" the believer.

To walk daily in the Holy Spirit is *to actively invite* the Holy Spirit to lead us, guide us, empower us, counsel us, and comfort us. We receive this daily work of the Holy Spirit in the same way that we received Jesus Christ as Savior—by our faith. We ask the Holy Spirit to fill us anew each morning and then believe that God is at work in us and through us all day long.

There are four vital aspects of walking in the Spirit that I believe are critical for us to teach our children:

1. The Holy Spirit wants us to be separated from everything that is contrary to God's will.

Paul identified a number of behaviors that are contrary to the will of God. In most cases, he identified what we are *not* to do, and also what we *are* to do. Here are some behaviors from Ephesians:

> "Putting away lying, each one speak truth with his neighbor" (4:25).

> "Let all bitterness, wrath, anger, clamor, and evil speaking be put away from you, with all malice. And be kind to one another, tenderhearted, forgiving one another, just as God in Christ also forgave you" (4:31–32).

୶ "But fornication and all uncleanness or covetousness, let it not even be named among you, as is fitting for saints; neither filthiness, nor foolish talking, nor coarse jesting, which are not fitting, but rather giving of thanks" (5:3–4).

୶ "Do not be drunk with wine, in which is dissipation; but be filled with the Spirit" (5:18).

୶ Make a list below of things which Paul tells us *not* to do in the above verses.

୶ Make a list below of things which Paul tells us *to* do.

2. We have a responsibility to yield ourselves entirely to Christ.

To yield to the Spirit means to transfer all control over one's possessions and use of talents, time, gifts, and resources to the Holy Spirit.
We must pray daily, "Holy Spirit, live Your life through me. Do not let
me say or do anything that is displeasing to You today. I yield all rights
of my life to You. Lead and guide me into what it is that You desire."

In failing to yield our lives to the Holy Spirit, we are assuming responsibility for our own lives and are attempting to live in our own strength,
wisdom, and power. In yielding our lives to the Spirit, we may still
make mistakes, because none of us is perfect, but we *can* be assured
that, even if we err or fall short of God's goal, the Lord will intercede on
our behalf and *complete* the work that He desires to do.

Jesus taught in Matthew 6:24:

> No one can serve two masters; for either he will hate the one
> and love the other, or else he will be loyal to the one and de-
> spise the other. You cannot serve God and mammon.

The Holy Spirit will not *demand* that we yield to Him. Yielding is a matter of our daily will. You can greatly influence how your child relates to
the Holy Spirit by teaching him to respect authority. You do this, in
part, by showing respect for authority in your own life. Each of us is
under authority to someone. The centurion who came to Jesus on behalf of his sick servant knew this (see Luke 7:1–10). Jesus Himself was
under the authority of the Father. Your child is under your authority as
long as you have responsibility for him. As Paul taught, "Children, obey
your parents in the Lord, for this is right" (Ephesians 6:1).

Do not allow your child to be disrespectful of those in authority over
him: teachers, pastors, Sunday school teachers, law-enforcement of-

ficials, or any other adult who bears responsibility for his welfare. A child who is allowed to show disrespect to parents and other adults will find it very difficult to yield all authority for his life to the Holy Spirit.

> Likewise you younger people, submit yourselves to your elders. Yes, all of you be submissive to one another, and be clothed with humility, for "GOD RESISTS THE PROUD, BUT GIVES GRACE TO THE HUMBLE."

> —1 Peter 5:5

☙ According to this verse, what is the best way for your child to learn how to be submissive?

☙ How well do you submit to others?

3. To be cleansed from all sin and yielded to the Holy Spirit results in a life of great joy!

To walk in the Spirit is not to walk through life with a long face, stooped shoulders, and a downcast expression. It is to walk in great exuberance. Paul encouraged the believers at Ephesus by calling them to "be filled with the Spirit, speaking to one another in psalms and hymns and spiritual songs, singing and making melody in your heart to the Lord, giving thanks always for all things to God the Father in the name of our Lord Jesus Christ" (Ephesians 5:18–20). The Christian life is intended to be a life of great joy—knowing that we are free of sin's bondage, guilt, and shame, and that Jesus promises us an "abundant life" on this earth and an "eternal home with God the Father."

Let your child hear you praise God often for the direction that the Holy Spirit is giving to your life and for the good things that you experience from His hand on a daily basis.

> Do not sorrow, for the joy of the LORD is your strength.

> —Nehemiah 8:10

~ What is the "joy of the Lord"?

~ In what ways can the "joy of the Lord" bring a person strength? Give practical examples.

4. As the Holy Spirit convicts us of sin, we must ask for immediate forgiveness.

To walk daily with the Holy Spirit means to walk in an ongoing state of cleansing and forgiveness. As the Holy Spirit brings things to our mind that are not right before God, our immediate impulse must be to ask God's forgiveness. It is as we do this that we truly walk in righteousness and holiness.

Our walk in the Holy Spirit leads us into goodness and blessing. It is a joyful walk of total dependence upon the Lord that allows us to live free of sin and to love God and others in purity. What a great legacy a child receives if he comes to accept Christ Jesus as his Savior, learns to say no to temptation, and learns how to walk daily in the Spirit!

> Blessed is the man who endures temptation; for when he has been approved, he will receive the crown of life which the Lord has promised to those who love Him.
>
> —James 1:12

☞ What does it mean to "endure" temptation?

෴ What blessing does this bring?

෴ Today and Tomorrow ෴

TODAY: THE FIRST AND MOST IMPORTANT STEP AS A CHRISTIAN PARENT IS TO LEAD MY CHILDREN TO CHRIST.

TOMORROW: I WILL SPEND TIME IN PRAYER, ASKING THE LORD TO TEACH ME THROUGH HIS HOLY SPIRIT.

෴ Notes and Prayer Requests: ෴

LESSON 6

Relating to Others in a Godly Way

---- ✑ **In This Lesson** ✑ ----

LEARNING: WHAT SHOULD I DO IF MY CHILDREN CAN'T GET ALONG WITH
OTHERS?

GROWING: WHAT ARE THE SECRETS TO GOOD RELATIONSHIPS?

✑

Every Christian parent has a desire for his children to get along with
other people—to be liked, appreciated, and respected by others. A parent gives a child a godly legacy in teaching him *how* to relate to other
people in a way that is pleasing to God. Paul identified characteristics
of the godly life—traits necessary for godly relationships. In this, lesson
we will focus on these aspects of the godly life:

  ✑ wholesome communication

  ✑ gentleness, kindness, and patience

  ✑ submission one to another

The principles that we will cover in the first two segments relate to *all*
relationships in life: those with believers in Christ Jesus and those with
unbelievers. The last segment, however, has a qualifier: We are only to
walk in *close fellowship* with other believers.

There are certain blessings in Christ that are reserved exclusively for those who walk in the Spirit. This does not mean that we are to live one way before non-believers and another before believers. That would be hypocrisy. We are to live as believers in Christ Jesus at all times, in all situations, regardless of circumstances or who is present. The Scriptures, however, admonish us not to be "yoked" with non-believers. This means that we must not be closely aligned with them or be "one" with them. Those who are yoked together are like oxen pulling in the same direction for the same cause toward the same goals in life. The non-believer is simply not going in the same direction as the believer! We cannot truly have unity with those who are not following Christ. We can respect them, show kindness to them, witness to them about Christ, but we cannot be in close fellowship with them.

We are to submit to those who have authority over us, including government officials who may not be righteous, but we are not to submit to their unrighteous ideas (which would result in our adopting those ideas as our own) or to their commands that would cause us to denounce our faith or bring disrepute upon Christ. Daniel is a great example of this. He was carried off to Babylon along with other righteous young Jews, and he found himself being asked to do things that were contrary to God's laws. We have Daniel's response to this situation in Daniel 1:8:

> But Daniel purposed in his heart that he would not defile himself with the portion of the king's delicacies, nor with the wine which he drank; therefore he requested of the chief of the eunuchs that he might not defile himself.

The result of his obedience to God was that "God gave them knowledge and skill in all literature and wisdom; and Daniel had understanding in all visions and dreams" (Daniel 1:17). Later, Nebuchadnezzar ordered everyone to bow down and worship a golden image that he had set up, with the threat of death in a fiery furnace to all who disobeyed. But

Daniel's friends—Shadrach, Meshach, and Abed-Nego—said this to the king (Daniel 3:16–18):

> O Nebuchadnezzar, we have no need to answer you in this matter. If that is the case, our God whom we serve is able to deliver us from the burning fiery furnace, and He will deliver us from your hand, O king. But if not, let it be known to you, O king, that we do not serve your gods, nor will we worship the gold image which you have set up.

Anytime that we do not submit to those in authority, we must be prepared to accept the consequences of our actions. Nevertheless, to submit to some people in their evil intent is to *reject God,* failing to submit to His commandments and authority—and that we must never do!

☙ Have you attempted to live in a "yoked" relationship with an ungodly person? What were the results?

☙ Daniel's friends were willing to die before they violated God's commands. How does this compare with your own attitude toward God's Word?

There are those who may think, "This sounds as if the Christian life is an exclusive life." No! All are invited by Christ Jesus to participate in His life. All are to be given an opportunity to know Him and to receive Him and to be forgiven and reconciled to God the Father. There is no exclusivity to "membership in Christ Jesus."

Once we are in Christ Jesus, however, we *are* to walk in "the straight and narrow." Are we free to do anything that we like in this life as Christians? No. We are to walk in a prescribed way of righteousness that is pleasing to God—a way that refrains from sin. Are we to think anything that we want to think? No. We *are* to be narrow-minded—our minds are to be focused on those things that are edifying and that bring glory to God. There are many things that we as believers are *not* to think about, imagine, or dwell upon in our minds (see Philippians 4:8–9).

We should always be presenting the Gospel to unbelievers and inviting them to accept Christ and become part of the Body of Christ. We are to be disciplined, focused, and bonded together with those of like mind in our pursuit of a godly life.

> Do not be unequally yoked together with unbelievers. For what fellowship has righteousness with lawlessness? And what communion has light with darkness? ... Therefore "COME OUT FROM AMONG THEM AND BE SEPARATE, SAYS THE LORD. DO NOT TOUCH WHAT IS UNCLEAN, AND I WILL RECEIVE YOU."
>
> —2 Corinthians 6:14, 17

∿ What are some examples of being "unequally yoked" with unbelievers?

∿ What does it mean to "come out from among them and be separate"?

☙ Give practical examples of what it means to "touch what is unclean". Do your children see you touching unclean things?

Wholesome Communication

The ways that we speak to other people establishes the relationship that we have with them. Our words also reveal the relationship that we *presently* have with another person, or which we have had in the past. Paul said this in Ephesians 4:29–31:

> Let no corrupt communication proceed out of your mouth, but what is good for necessary edification, that it may impart grace to the hearers. And do not grieve the Holy Spirit of God, by whom you were sealed for the day of redemption. Let all bitterness, wrath, anger, clamor, and evil speaking be put away from you, with all malice.

Later in his letter to the Ephesians, Paul calls upon them not to engage in "foolish talking, nor coarse jesting" (5:4). "Corrupt" words might be considered unwholesome words. They are words that are unfit, worthless, rotten, and corrupting by nature—words that cause distrust of God, disrepute of other people, and disharmony in a body of believers. They are words that ultimately hurt the speaker as much as the hearer. At times, it is not *what* we say that corrupts as much as *how* we speak. Words spoken in anger, derision, or bitterness cannot produce good fruit in another person's life.

 When have you felt yourself "corrupted" by what someone said to you? When have you made a comment that caused harm to someone else?

> Finally, brethren, whatever things are true, ... noble, ... just, ... pure, ... lovely, ... of good report, if there is any virtue and if there is anything praiseworthy—meditate on these things.
>
> —Philippians 4:8

 List examples of each of the following qualities:

True:

Just:

Pure:

Lovely:

Good report:

When we engage in ungodly communication, we "grieve" the Holy Spirit. It is impossible to grieve someone who doesn't love you. The Holy Spirit loves us so much and desires so many blessings for us that He is grieved when we speak in an ungodly manner, because what we say reflects the attitude of our heart. Jesus taught, "Out of the abundance of the heart the mouth speaks. A good man out of the good treasure of his heart brings forth good things, and an evil man out of the evil treasure brings forth evil things . . . For by your words you will be justified, and by your words you will be condemned" (Matthew 12:34–35, 37).

Godly communication edifies other people—builds them up, encourages them, is helpful to them. We are to speak positive, life-giving, God-honoring words to others, and we are to do so in a way that is timely, addressing the need of the moment.

Monitor your own speech—your child may very well be repeating what you are saying! Guard your tongue. Discipline your child regarding his speech, just as you would any other form of behavior. What we say is just as important before God as any other form of behavior!

> Out of the same mouth proceed blessing and cursing. My brethren, these things ought not to be so. Does a spring send forth fresh water and bitter from the same opening?
>
> —James 3:10-11

❧ When have you caught yourself praising God with one breath, then cursing someone (literally or figuratively) with the next?

☜ When have you heard your children repeating things that you said? Were those things good or not so good?

Gentleness, Kindness, and Patience

Throughout the New Testament, we find believers called to be gentle, kind, and patient. To do so is to reflect the very nature of God! Paul wrote that "the fruit of the Spirit is love, joy, peace, *longsuffering*, *kindness*, goodness, faithfulness, *gentleness*, self-control" (Galatians 5:22–23, *emphasis added*).

No person is born to be gentle, kind, or patient. These attributes are not part of our inborn nature. We must *learn* to be gentle, kind, and patient—and it is the responsibility of a parent to teach a child these *behavior traits* until they are automatic and become *character traits*. We teach these behaviors through repeated training—insisting that a child act with gentleness, rewarding him for kindness, and reminding him to be patient. And, at all times, we are to treat our child with kindness, gentleness, and patience. There is no excuse from God's point of view for a parent who abuses a child, is harsh with a child, or who loses his temper with a child.

Kindness, gentleness, and patience require great discipline and self-control on the part of any person, including any child. We must ask the Lord daily to help us control our desires and impulses, and to "put them under the bridle" of the Holy Spirit.

63

He who is slow to anger is better than the mighty, And he who rules his spirit than he who takes a city.

—Proverbs 16:32

∽ What does it mean to "rule your spirit"? How is this done in practical terms?

∽ What is required for a man to conquer a fortified city? How do these qualities compare with the effort involved in controlling your own anger?

Submission to One Another

Submission is rooted in two key words: *humility* and *trust*. Believers are to submit to other believers *because we together are in Christ Jesus*. We are subject to God, and therefore we are to be in a position of humility before God. Being humble does not mean being a "doormat." It means bowing before God in awe, respect, and worship to say, "I am your servant. I will do whatever You tell me to do." If we see ourselves as servants of God, we are able to be what Christ calls us to be—a servant to others.

Humility is not having an inferiority complex. It is not saying, "I am a nobody" or "I'm not worth anything." Rather, it is saying, "I am in submission to God." The Greeks and the Romans had no use for the word *humility*—to them, it was a "slave" word. Only slaves were "humble." To the Christian, being humble was to be under the bridle of God, to be made useful and desirable from God's perspective. We see humility in John the Baptist—who was never a shy, retiring wimp—when he said of Jesus, "There stands One among you whom you do not know. It is He who, coming after me, is preferred before me, whose sandal strap I am not worthy to loose" (John 1:26–27).

Trust is a second key ingredient. When we submit ourselves to others, we are yielding the authority of decision-making to that other person. It is only because we are trusting God to work in our life and in the life of the person over us that we are able to submit to the decisions that another person makes. The believer is called to trust God—and only God—to work *all* things together for our eternal good. Of one thing we can be assured: when we submit ourselves to others in humility and trust God, *He* will reward us.

> Remind them to be subject to rulers and authorities, to obey, to be ready for every good work.
>
> —Titus 3:1

➤ What is required "to be ready for every good work"?

✎ Why do we need to be "reminded" of this teaching frequently? What is the best way to remind your children of this principle?

In teaching our children how to communicate in a godly way with others; how to treat others with gentleness, kindness, and patience; and how to submit to others in ways that are pleasing to God, we are preparing them to lead godly lives and to establish godly homes, godly business partnerships, and godly communities. What a wonderful legacy to be taught *how* to have good relationships! The person who treats others in a godly way is respected and admired, even in times of disagreement.

> Let your speech always be with grace, seasoned with salt, that you may know how you ought to answer each one.
>
> —Colossians 4:6

✎ What does it mean, in practical terms, to "let your speech always be seasoned with grace"?

❧ What are the qualities of salt? How can these qualities be reflected in your speech?

❧ Today and Tomorrow ❧

TODAY: MY SPEECH, AS WELL AS MY ACTIONS, SHOULD REFLECT THE CHARACTER OF CHRIST AT ALL TIMES.

TOMORROW: I WILL WORK TO SEASON MY LIFE WITH GENTLENESS AND KINDNESS, AND WILL STRIVE TO SUBMIT TO OTHERS IN HUMILITY.

❧ Notes and Prayer Requests: ❧

LESSON 7

A Growing Relationship with the Lord

─── ✍ **In This Lesson** ✍ ───

LEARNING: HOW CAN I HELP MY CHILDREN NOW SO THAT THEY WILL CON-
TINUE TO GROW IN THE LORD ALL THEIR LIVES?

GROWING: WHAT PART DOES PRAYER PLAY IN THESE THINGS?

─── ∞ ───

The greatest inheritance that you can leave your child is a spiritual inheritance—salvation and the assurance of a heavenly home, followed
by a desire and an understanding about what it means to *grow* in one's
relationship with the Lord. Our salvation is secured by believing in the
Lord Jesus Christ as Savior and receiving the forgiveness that God the
Father makes available through Him. No other actions or deeds are
required. As Jesus said in John 6:29, 40:

> This is the work of God, that you believe in Him whom He sent
> ... And this is the will of Him who sent Me, that everyone who
> sees the Son and believes in Him may have everlasting life; and
> I will raise him up at the last day.

Salvation is the step that establishes the most important relationship
that your child will ever know—a relationship with God Almighty. It is,
however, only the first step in that relationship. Our relationship with
the Lord is expected to become richer, deeper, and more intimate every day, from the day of our salvation to the day we die. That happens

through prayer and spending time with the Lord, listening to what He says to us. *Teach* your child to pray.

How a Child Learns to Pray

A child learns to pray in these four ways:

I. A child mimics the way that his parents pray—in both terminology and attitude.

Pray with and for your child, allowing him to hear your spontaneous, personal prayers; otherwise, your child isn't going to pray. He is going to expect prayer only from a pastor's lips in a church setting. On the other hand, if you are quick to pray—any time, any place, about anything—your child will see that prayer is a normal part of everyday life, and he will be quick to pray. Your child will pray the way that *you* pray—he will copy your words, your phrases, and your posture.

&. What has been your experience with prayer? How did you learn to pray?

&. Who do you "mimic" when you pray—who was your prayer teacher?

69

In addition, your child will copy your attitude toward God as you pray. Children are quick to pick up the attitudes and emotions of the adults around them. *What* you say to God is going to be interpreted by *how* you say it. If your attitude is that God is a harsh judge just waiting to pronounce punishment upon you, your child will pick up on that attitude and approach God the same way, with fear and caution.

On the other hand, if your attitude is that God is a loving heavenly Father who is delighted to bless, guide, and help His children, your child will approach God with the same attitude—one marked by joy, vulnerability, and familiarity. If you consider prayer a duty and an obligation, your child will regard prayer the same way. If you approach prayer as a delight and a privilege, your child will approach prayer eagerly.

If you don't know God yourself, or if you see Him as distant and uninvolved in your life, your child will approach God as a stranger. If you have developed an intimate relationship with God, your child will approach God as Friend. If you pray with stilted, formal language, your child will regard prayer as a formal occasion. If you pray in everyday language, your child will be quick to pray in his own childlike terms.

❧ What is your attitude—your emotions—as you pray?

☙ How do you speak to God? Do you use a special "prayer language" or normal, everyday speech? Do you kneel?

2. What you pray for will be what your child prays for.

If you only pray about important things or in times of crisis, your child is likely to pray only about major events, desires, and problems in his life. If you pray about virtually *everything*, your child is going to regard prayer as a normal, ongoing conversation with God. Your child will come to believe that he can talk to God about *anything*.

Encourage your child to pray for his daily needs. A child who sees God as the Provider of all good things can trust God in all situations to do what is right and good. Encourage your child to pray for a daily forgiveness of his sins. A child who believes that God forgives freely and frequently will be free from abiding guilt and shame. Such a child is much more quick to receive the Lord Jesus as Savior and to invite the Holy Spirit to come into his life. Encourage your child also to forgive others and to pray especially for those who may be persecuting him.

Encourage your child to pray specifically for those in positions of leadership and authority, and to pray for pastors, missionaries, and all who proclaim the gospel of Jesus Christ, as well as for Christians in other countries who are going through times of persecution. In praying for other believers, your child will have a growing awareness of the Body of Christ around the world and a growing compassion for lost souls.

Therefore I exhort first of all that supplications, prayers, intercessions, and giving of thanks be made for all men, for kings
and all who are in authority, that we may lead a quiet and
peaceable life in all godliness and reverence.

—1 Timothy 2:1-2

Define each of the following types of prayer, with examples:

Supplications:

Intercessions:

Giving thanks:

How often do you pray each type of prayer? How often do you
include your children in those times of prayer?

3. What your child hears you pray on his behalf will have great impact on his life.

If your prayers are vague on your child's behalf—"Oh God, bless little Johnny, be with little Mary today"—your child is going to have fairly vague feelings about God's involvement in his life. On the other hand, if your prayers are specific—"Father, help Johnny with his math test today, give him a clear mind and an ability to concentrate and do his best, and give Mary the courage to smile and walk boldly when unkind children tease her"—your child is going to see God as being actively involved and of personal help every hour of his day. A child who is sent off to school every morning with prayer on his behalf is going to be much better equipped to withstand temptation, have courage in the face of difficulty, feel confident in the love of God, and be quicker to act on what is right in God's eyes.

One of the greatest teachers about prayer was the apostle Paul. He taught *by example*. He opens several of his letters with prayers. As you read through a few of these below, think how it must have felt for the early Christian believers to receive these letters and to hear what Paul was praying on their behalf. How encouraging his words would have been to them—and are to us today!

> I thank my God upon every remembrance of you, always in every prayer of mine making request for you all with joy, for your fellowship in the gospel from the first day until now, being confident of this very thing, that He who has begun a good work in you will complete it until the day of Jesus Christ;
>
> —Philippians 1:3-6

73

For this reason we also ... do not cease to pray for you, and to
ask that you may be filled with the knowledge of His will in all
wisdom and spiritual understanding; that you may walk worthy of the Lord, fully pleasing Him, being fruitful in every good
work and increasing in the knowledge of God; strengthened
with all might, according to His glorious power, for all patience
and longsuffering with joy; giving thanks to the Father who
has qualified us to be partakers of the inheritance of the saints
in the light.

—Colossians 1:9-12

What specific things does Paul pray for in these passages?

What specific things do you pray for your children?

4. A child whose prayers are invited begins to grow in his own relationship with God.

Pray *with* your child. Invite your child to voice his own petitions to God and to pray about whatever he desires, whenever he feels a need to pray. Never criticize the words that your child uses in prayer. Allow him free expression before God—after all, God looks on the heart, not at vocabulary.

Ask your child to pray about specific needs in your family and, from time to time, to pray for you about specific issues that you are facing or problems that you have. This is not to say that you should burden your child with all the details of your troubles or make him feel responsible for your problems. Rather, it is to *invite* your child to participate more fully in your life and to build a relationship "in the Spirit" with him. Such a relationship is highly valued by a child, and especially so as he becomes a parent himself one day.

Encourage your child in the fact that he has been given faith by God (Romans 12:3). Teach your child to pray with *faith* that God hears prayers, answers prayers, and that God will use your prayers to bring about an eternal benefit in his life and in the lives of others. Furthermore, in inviting your child to pray for you and for others in your family, you are expressing that you love your child and that he belongs to your family. You are expressing appreciation for your child's *spiritual* nature and your belief that God desires an ever-growing relationship with him.

When is a child old enough to pray for himself or to pray for other people? As soon as he can talk! "But what if God does not answer my child's prayer. How can I explain that?" God always answers the prayer of a sincere heart—He just may not answer in the way that we *want* Him to answer. God's answers to us are "yes," "no," "not at this time," and "if certain conditions are met." Teach your child that a "no" answer from God is still an answer, and that it is the *best* answer at this time from a loving heavenly Father, even if we don't understand why.

Teach your child about the power of agreement in prayer—if any two believers ask something of our heavenly Father, He will answer their prayer according to His will, which is always for our eternal benefit.

> "Again I say to you that if two of you agree on earth concerning anything that they ask, it will be done for them by My Father in heaven. For where two or three are gathered together in My name, I am there in the midst of them."
>
> —Matthew 18:19-20

⚘ According to these verses, why is it important that you spend time praying together with your child?

⚘ This week, start a prayer journal with your children. Write down dates and requests, leaving room for the date of the answer.

Praise and Thanksgiving

Throughout the Scriptures, we are encouraged to approach God with praise and thanksgiving. Praise and thanksgiving are to become the foundational attitude of our lives as believers in Christ. The person with an attitude of praise and thanksgiving stands in humility before God, quick to acknowledge "I cannot, but You can do all things." To have an attitude of praise and thanksgiving to God is to develop an attitude of gratitude for all that a person is given. What a wonderful legacy it is for a child to regard all of life as a gift from a loving Father—a gift to be cherished, used wisely, and enjoyed fully.

Every prayer that we voice should begin and end with thanksgiving and praise. When Jesus taught His disciples to pray in Matthew 6:9, 13, He taught them to begin and end their prayer with praise:

"Our Father in heaven, Hallowed be Your name."

"For Yours is the kingdom and the power and the glory forever."

Let your child hear you voice praise and thanksgiving often, every day. Praise God for the little things as well as the big things. Praise God for what He has done and for who He is—our loving, merciful, forgiving heavenly Father who delights in being our Provider, Sustainer, Deliverer, Counselor, Friend, and Protector. When we praise and thank God, we open our lives to Him in a way that allows us to receive even more of His blessings and to experience even more joy in His presence. The more praise and thanksgiving we voice with our prayers, the greater the peace and assurance we have that God will act on our behalf.

Be anxious for nothing, but in everything by prayer and supplication, with thanksgiving, let your requests be made known to
God; and the peace of God, which surpasses all understanding,
will guard your hearts and minds through Christ Jesus.

—Philippians 4:6-7

&. According to these verses, what is the cure for anxiety?

&. What do prayer and thanksgiving have to do with guarding our
hearts and minds? How can you begin to guard your children's
hearts and minds this way?

Developing a Listening Heart

In addition to voicing petitions and praise and thanksgiving to God, encourage your child to spend time listening to God. God speaks continually to His people, but those who are listening for His voice tend to hear what He says to them. God speaks in a still, small voice to our hearts, and it is up to each of us to open our spiritual ears and listen intently. Every time you read the Bible with your child, begin your time with prayer, inviting the Holy Spirit to speak to your hearts the truth of God's Word and to help you understand the message that God has for you.

Teach your child that God speaks words of encouragement and edification to the heart. God causes us to feel convicted about our sins—not so that we might fear punishment, but so that we might ask for God's forgiveness. Above all, God speaks to us of His great love for us. What a wonderful legacy it is for your child to learn to hear from God for himself—to trust in God, to turn quickly to God in every situation, to receive God's assurance and love, and to know without doubt that God is present with him always!

> Enter into His gates with thanksgiving, And into His courts with praise. Be thankful to Him, and bless His name. For the LORD is good; His mercy is everlasting, And His truth endures to all generations.
>
> —Psalm 100:4-5

✎ What does it mean to "enter into His gates" and "into His courts"? Why are we to begin these things with thanksgiving and praise?

🐟 Make a list below of things that you are thankful for. Then ask your children what they are thankful for, and add those items to the list.

🐟 Today and Tomorrow 🐟

TODAY: MY CHILD WILL LEARN TO PRAY BY IMITATING THE WAY THAT I PRAY.

TOMORROW: I WILL SPEND TIME THIS WEEK LISTENING TO GOD, AND I WILL INCLUDE MY CHILDREN IN MY TIMES OF PRAYER.

🐟 Notes and Prayer Requests: 🐟

Lesson 8

A High Value upon God's Word

☙ In This Lesson ☙

LEARNING: WHAT VALUE DOES THE BIBLE HAVE IN THE LIVES OF MY CHILDREN?

GROWING: HOW CAN I PERSUADE MY CHILDREN TO READ THE BIBLE?

If you were able to give your child the *best,* most beneficial, and wisest advice in the world—at all times throughout his life—you would no doubt feel that you were an excellent parent. The fact is, you *can* give your child such advice by teaching him to read the Bible and to turn *first* to the Bible for answers to life's problems, needs, and questions.

The Scriptures command us to *teach* God's Word to our children. This is not solely the responsibility of a pastor or a Sunday school teacher. It is every parent's responsibility to make certain that his child knows God's Word. Note the commandment from Deuteronomy 6:4–9:

> Hear, O Israel: The LORD our God, the LORD is one! You shall love the LORD your God with all your heart, with all your soul, and with all your might. And these words which I command you today shall be in your heart. You shall teach them diligently to your children, and shall talk of them when you sit in your house, when you walk by the way, when you lie down, and

when you rise up. You shall bind them as a sign on your hand, and they shall be as frontlets between your eyes. You shall write them on the doorposts of your house and on your gates.

The Word of God is to become the very perspective of our lives—we are to see the world through the lens of God's Word. God's truth is to be the motivation for all that we do—everything that we say and do should become a reflection of God's Word. God's truth is to reign supreme in our homes. Anyone who is around our family should recognize that God's truth is the "law" for our family, the rule that we live by, and the code of conduct that we strive to uphold. Furthermore, we are to teach God's Word in a natural way to our children, from morning to night, as we talk about things that we encounter and as we reflect upon various circumstances in our lives.

God's Word is a spiritual document, and it is learned in the *spirit* of your child. God's Word must become the foundation on which your child's *conscience* is built. It must be the "right way" to live and to believe.

☙ How did you learn right from wrong? On what did you base your understanding?

82

And now, Israel, what does the LORD your God require of you, but to fear the LORD your God, to walk in all His ways and to love Him, to serve the LORD your God with all your heart and with all your soul, and to keep the commandments of the LORD and His statutes which I command you today for your good?

—Deuteronomy 10:12-13

☙ What does it mean to serve God "with all your heart and with all your soul"? What is the difference between heart and soul?

How a Child Learns God's Word

A child learns God's Word in three important ways:

I. Your child learns God's Word and begins to appreciate it through your reading it aloud.

Reading gives a child an awareness of language, broadens his horizons, creates a love for learning, and gives him a feeling of closeness to the parent who is reading to him. When a parent reads God's Word—usually in the form of Bible stories at the beginning of his life—that parent builds into a child all of the benefits of reading with these added advantages: an awareness of God's presence, an understanding about how God works and why we must obey God, and a feeling of closeness to God.

Always uphold to your child the *importance* of God's Word—that it is the truth of God, the way that we are to live, and that it is for our benefit now and forever. The Bible is not "just another story"—it is *the* book of books.

> My son, keep my words, And treasure my commands within you. Keep my commands and live, And my law as the apple of your eye. Bind them on your fingers; Write them on the tablet of your heart. Say to wisdom, "You are my sister," And call understanding your nearest kin.
>
> —Proverbs 7:1-4

What does it mean to bind the commands of God on your fingers? To "write them on the tablet of your heart"?

☙ How can these visual images help your child understand the importance of God's Word:

Treasure:

Apple of your eye:

Bound around your fingers:

Written on the tablet of your heart:

Wisdom is my sister:

Understanding is my closest relative:

2. Your child learns God's Word by memorizing Scripture.

Even when your child may not understand all of the vocabulary words or the full meaning of a verse, he *can* memorize God's Word. When the Word is hidden away in a child's lasting memory, the Holy Spirit can bring God's truth to mind at precisely the time it is needed most. What a child hasn't learned, the Holy Spirit cannot recall!

When your child memorizes God's Word, he also establishes the truth of God as part of the very way that he *thinks* and acts. When the truth of God becomes the *first* or *foundational* way that a child thinks, he will always have a God-first perspective on life, understanding that what God says matters.

> My son, if you receive my words, And treasure my commands within you, So that you incline your ear to wisdom, And apply your heart to understanding; Yes, if you cry out for discernment, And lift up your voice for understanding, If you seek her as silver, And search for her as for hidden treasures; Then you will understand the fear of the LORD, And find the knowledge of God.
>
> —Proverbs 2:1-5

Consider the verbs in these verses, giving practical definitions for each:

Receive:

Treasure:

Incline your ear:

Apply your heart:

Cry out:

Lift up your voice:

Seek:

Search:

🕭 Why do these verses suggest that finding wisdom is hard work? How can these verses help your child become wise?

3. A child learns God's Word by reading and studying it.

As soon as your child is able to read, encourage the reading of God's Word. Buy a translation of the Bible that your child can understand. Many Bibles have study notes for children and young adults. Encourage your child to go to the Bible to discover answers to questions about life. Show your child how to use a concordance, a Bible dictionary, and various other Bible-study helps. Actively explore—*together*—the Bible's answers to specific problems that your child faces. The more your child sees the Bible as applicable and beneficial to his own life, the quicker he will be to turn to the Bible for God's answers.

Your child will benefit greatly from seeing *you* reading the Bible often and by seeing *you* go to the Bible for answers in your own life. A love of God's Word comes to your child as he sees you valuing God's Word!

> All Scripture is given by inspiration of God, and is profitable for doctrine, for reproof, for correction, for instruction in righteousness, that the man of God may be complete, thoroughly equipped for every good work.
>
> —2 Timothy 3:16-17

Define each of the following words, giving practical examples of each:

Doctrine:

Reproof:

Correction:

Instruction:

In what ways, practically speaking, is a person "incomplete" and "unequipped" for life without the Bible? How does this apply to your children?

Believe What You Read!

Children encounter a great deal in our world today that is imaginary or mythical. Encourage your child always to approach God's Word as lasting, eternal, rock-solid truth. The Bible presents what is pleasing and desired by God—it tells how to relate to God, how to relate to others, and how to have peace of heart. It is the key to all understanding about human nature, God's nature, and about spiritual reality.

God does not want us to live in a state of confusion or darkness. The very opposite is true! He desires that we walk in wisdom, knowing what is good, right, and helpful. We are to know truth, to walk in truth, and to speak truth! Furthermore, God expects us to act upon what we read. We are to *do* God's Word—live out His truth, express His message to others, and be witnesses to the gospel of Jesus Christ. We are to live what we believe. We are not called simply to "talk the talk" of God's Word, but to "walk the walk."

> The entirety of Your word is truth, And every one of Your righteous judgments endures forever.
>
> —Psalms 119:160

What does this verse suggest about our approach to reading the Bible? How can you include "the entirety" of God's Word in reading to your children?

89

❧ Keep a record below of the Scripture passages that you read with your children in the coming week. Use this as a starting point to read through the entire Bible together over the next year.

Finally, God's Word has been given to us for our benefit. His Word is *life*-giving—it shows us how we can receive eternal life through God's Son, and helps us recognize God's blessings. God's commandments are not given to us to "take away our fun" or to put us in a spiritual strait-jacket; they are given to us for our protection, so that we might receive all of the good things that God desires. Encourage your child to believe what the Word says and to do what the Word commands—and also to look for the blessing that comes from believing and obeying God's Word! A child will always have access to wise counsel when he knows where to go for answers in times of doubt or trouble, when he needs problem-solving and decision-making advice.

But be doers of the word, and not hearers only, deceiving your-selves.

—James 1:22

☙ In what ways do we deceive ourselves if we are "hearers only" of God's Word? How can you help your child understand this?

☙ In what areas in your own life do you tend to be a "hearer" rather than a "doer"? How might your children be imitating this pattern?

Great peace have those who love Your law, And nothing causes them to stumble.

—Psalms 119:165

❧ Why does loving God's Word keep a person from stumbling?

❧ How will you increase your children's love of God's Word?

❧ Today and Tomorrow ❧

TODAY: MY CHILDREN WILL ONLY LEARN TO LOVE GOD'S WORD IF I READ IT MYSELF—AND READ IT WITH THEM.

TOMORROW: I WILL BEGIN A DAILY PLAN OF READING THE BIBLE WITH MY CHILDREN.

LESSON 9

Overcoming Problems and Unpleasant Situations

———— ❧ In This Lesson ☙ ————

LEARNING: WHAT IS THE DIFFERENCE BETWEEN "PROBLEMS" AND "UN-
PLEASANT SITUATIONS"?

GROWING: HOW CAN I TEACH MY CHILDREN TO OVERCOME BOTH?

Christians are not immune from problems and trials. We all encounter unpleasant circumstances from time to time. One of the greatest gifts that any parent can give a child is an ability to recognize the true source of all problems, to face problems squarely in the power of the Holy Spirit.

The world in which Paul lived was filled with problems and unpleasant situations. The majority of people in his day were slaves living in cities that had been occupied by Rome. Paul's epistles were addressed to churches that consisted largely of slaves. Paul himself was never a slave to a human master. However, he frequently referred to himself as a bondservant of Jesus Christ—he saw himself in total submission to his master and lord.

Paul never taught that a person should *like* being a slave, but he did teach that a person can be content in any condition and that a believer in Christ Jesus can live as a "free person" (see 1 Peter 2:15–16). Paul's teaching for how to live victoriously in unpleasant situations is at the heart of this lesson.

> ...I have learned in whatever state I am, to be content: I know how to be abased, and I know how to abound. Everywhere and in all things I have learned both to be full and to be hungry, both to abound and to suffer need. I can do all things through Christ who strengthens me.
>
> —Philippians 4:11-13

∾ Notice that Paul says that he has "learned" to be content. How is this lesson learned?

∾ How much contentment do your children see in your own attitudes? If they grow up imitating you, how likely are they to find contentment?

You can promise your child that those who believe in Christ Jesus will live forever with the Lord, but never promise him that he will grow up to live "happily ever after" in this lifetime. You can promise your child that God has great blessings for him in his future, but never promise him that he will live a life free of problems and struggles. You can promise your child that God will meet all of his *needs* according to the riches of Christ Jesus, but never promise him that God is going to give him everything that he *wants*.

Life has ups and downs, good times and bad times. To be taught otherwise is to live in fantasy. The good news is that we have the Holy Spirit to help us in our times of trouble. We always have the hope of heaven before us, and we can always *choose* to have a joyful attitude, no matter how difficult, painful, or stressful a situation may be.

> ...we also glory in tribulations, knowing that tribulation produces perseverance; and perseverance, character; and character, hope.

> —Romans 5:3-4

≈ Give practical examples of how tribulation produces perseverance, and how perseverance produces character.

≈ Why does character produce hope? Why are these qualities important in your children's lives?

Two Key Principles for Overcoming the Unpleasant

Paul placed emphasis on two key principles in overcoming the unpleasant: obedience and diligence.

1. *We are always to remain obedient to God and to those that He has placed in authority over us, even in unpleasant situations.* Paul wrote this to the slaves in the church at Ephesus (Ephesians 6:5–8):

> Servants, be obedient to those who are your masters according to the flesh, with fear and trembling, in sincerity of heart, as to Christ; not with eyeservice, as men-pleasers, but as servants of Christ, doing the will of God from the heart, with good will doing service, as to the Lord, and not to men, knowing that whatever good anyone does, he will receive the same from the Lord, whether he is a slave or free.

There is no substitute for *doing* what is required of us. We are not to *say* that we will fulfill an obligation only if it suits us to keep our word. We are to *do* what we commit ourselves to do and to obey those who require service of us. Children are required to obey their parents; servants are required to obey their masters; and all of us are to obey those in spiritual and political authority over us with this attitude: *as to the Lord*. In other words, we are to obey as if God Himself is in charge of our lives—which truly is the case!

Jesus gave an illustration of the importance of our obedience in Matthew 21:28–31:

> "A man had two sons, and he came to the first and said, 'Son, go, work today in my vineyard.' He answered and said, 'I will not,' but afterward he regretted it and went. Then he came to the second and said likewise. And he answered and said, 'I go,

sir,' but he did not go. Which of the two did the will of his father?"

They said to Him, "The first."

Obedience enables us to receive God's help and reward. In good times and bad, we must obey what God has commanded, regardless of how we feel or how others behave.

🙠 In the Ephesians passage above, what does it mean to obey "with eyeservice"? When have you seen this behavior in your own children?

🙠 What principle was Jesus teaching in the Matthew passage above?

2. We are to be diligent in our work and in our witness for Christ, even in difficult situations. Being diligent first means being *willing* to work hard. When people are faced with an unpleasant task or a difficult situation, they behave in one of these three ways: they avoid the situation as much as possible; they complain bitterly about the situation; or they do the minimal effort required in hopes of getting through the situation as quickly as possible.

The Bible presents a different approach: work as if you are being paid or rewarded twice—once by the person in authority over you, and once by God. There is no justification for doing half-hearted work or for producing poor quality workmanship. God sees what we do, even if nobody else does, and He sees and rewards what we do as well as our attitude while doing it.

> And whatever you do in word or deed, do all in the name of the Lord Jesus, giving thanks to God the Father through Him.
>
> —Colossians 3:17

Give practical examples from your own life of ways that you can "do all in the name of the Lord Jesus".

🐚 Give practical examples of ways that you can teach this principle to your children.

A reward is held out to all who obey and are diligent in the face of unpleasant tasks or commandments that aren't to our liking. Jesus said that those who are faithful over little will be given much to rule over in the future. Those who are obedient bring the Lord joy. If you truly want to delight the heart of God, obey Him! (See Matthew 25:23.)

This means that we are to *require* obedience from our children and refuse to accept or wink at their disobedience. We are to require that our children give full effort to the things that they undertake, doing so with a cheerful attitude all the way to the completion of the task—even if that task has unpleasant aspects. Parents must:

🐚 *Discipline children with love.* In this, they teach a child respect for others, respect for themselves, and ultimately respect for God.

🐚 *Be consistent in what they require of a child.* This teaches a child what it means to be steadfast and faithful.

🐚 *Only require what God requires.* At no time are we to put a burden on our child that is beyond what God requires solely.

And you, fathers, do not provoke your children to wrath, but
bring them up in the training and admonition of the Lord.

—Ephesians 6:4

☙ Give practical examples of ways that a parent might provoke
his children to wrath.

☙ What is "the training and admonition of the Lord"? How does
a parent bring up children that way?

Problems versus Unpleasant Situations

We are to teach our children the difference between a problem and something that is uncomfortable or unpleasant. Sin and evil are the source of all problems. The unjust persecution of God's people is also a problem in God's eyes.

∞ The Solution to Sin-Related Problems ∞

The solution to problems that arise from our own sin is confession of that sin to God, and repentance—which is a change of our heart and behavior. If we have hurt others by what we have said or done, we are also to ask their forgiveness and to make amends as best we can.

> I acknowledged my sin to You, And my iniquity I have not hidden. I said, "I will confess my transgressions to the LORD," And You forgave the iniquity of my sin.
>
> —Psalm 32:5

∞ When have you tried to hide your own sin? When have your children discovered them just the same?

∽. When you lose your temper or hurt your child, how often do you apologize to him? What is the relation between confessing sin to God and asking forgiveness from others?

∽ The Solution to Persecution-Related Problems ∽

When your child is being treated unfairly by others, the solution lies in prayer, trusting God, and doing good to the persecutor.

First, we are to pray that God will deliver us from those who persecute us (see Psalm 142:6). Second, we are to leave any vengeance or acts of retaliation up to God (see Romans 12:19). Those who persecute us become "enemies" of the Lord, and to be an enemy of the Lord is to be in a very undesirable position (see Deuteronomy 32:43 and Nahum 1:2). Third, we are to act in a positive way toward those who persecute us until God delivers us. Read what Jesus said in Matthew 5:44–45 about dealing with our persecutors:

> But I say to you, love your enemies, bless those who curse you, do good to those who hate you, and pray for those who spitefully use you and persecute you, that you may be sons of your Father in heaven.

Finally, teach your child that persecution related to faith in Christ is inevitable. Prepare your child for such persecution, which may come in the form of rejection, ridicule, teasing, or bullying. Encourage your child that his endurance of any persecution related to his faith results in a great reward from God. Jesus taught in Matthew 5:10:

> Blessed are those who are persecuted for righteousness' sake,
> For theirs is the kingdom of heaven.

☞ When have you been persecuted for your faith in God? When have your children been persecuted for their faith?

☞ How do you respond to people who treat you badly? What situations are your children presently facing that can serve as lessons in loving their enemies?

∞ The Solution for Satan-Created Problems. ∞

In addition to the problems created by our own sin and by our persecutors, there are problems directly created by Satan. Satan works through
persecutors and through evil people to create negative situations in our
lives. We must be quick to recognize that a person who is hurting us is
not the real source of the problem—Satan is the source. These spiritual problems are intended to destroy us and demolish our witness for
Christ. The solution, spiritual warfare, is described by Paul in Ephesians 6:10–13:

> Finally, my brethren, be strong in the Lord and in the power
> of His might. Put on the whole armor of God, that you may be
> able to stand against the wiles of the devil. For we do not wres-
> tle against flesh and blood, but against principalities, against
> powers, against the rulers of the darkness of this age, against
> spiritual hosts of wickedness in the heavenly places. Therefore
> take up the whole armor of God, that you may be able to with-
> stand in the evil day, and having done all, to stand.

Paul's description of the whole armor of God is a wonderful picture
of Christ in us. The armor that we are putting on is the very nature of
Christ. He is our truth, our righteousness, our peace, the source of our
faith, the author of our salvation, and the living Word spoken by God.

> Stand therefore, having girded your waist with truth, having
> put on the breastplate of righteousness, and having shod your
> feet with the preparation of the gospel of peace; above all, tak-
> ing the shield of faith with which you will be able to quench all
> the fiery darts of the wicked one. And take the helmet of salva-
> tion, and the sword of the Spirit, which is the word of God.

> —Ephesians 6:14–17

🖎 Describe how each piece of armor is worn and what it does:

Belt:

Breastplate:

Shoes:

Shield:

Helmet:

Sword:

🖎 Give practical examples of each piece of armor, and how you and your children can use them this week.

Once we have put on the armor of God, the nature of Christ Jesus, we are to *stand*—to endure, to refuse to be moved from our position of righteousness, to refuse to give in to temptation—and we are to *pray*. Paul's conclusion to putting on the whole armor is this: "praying always with all prayer and supplication in the Spirit, being watchful to this end with all perseverance and supplication for all the saints" (Ephesians 6:18). We are to call on the name of the Lord and pray for His deliverance. We are to ask Him to defeat the devil in our lives and to act in victorious strength and power on our behalf.

You may be asking, "Can a child engage in spiritual warfare?" Yes! A child can be taught from the earliest age to put on the whole armor of God and to resist the devil. We are wise to teach our children how to put on the armor of God in a way that is literal to them—imagining that they are putting on a helmet, a breastplate, and so forth as they recite and memorize Ephesians 6:14–17. In this way, they feel stronger in their faith and more courageous as they face the world each day, and they have a visual image to help them remember all their lives that their strength lies totally in Christ Jesus. Furthermore, your child *can* resist the devil and *can* pray! Even a young child can be taught to pray, "Help me, God!"

Encourage your child that, as he resists the devil, the devil *must* flee from him (see James 4:7). Encourage your child also that Jesus is the Deliverer from all evil, all the time.

Therefore submit to God. Resist the devil and he will flee from you. Draw near to God and He will draw near to you. Cleanse your hands, you sinners; and purify your hearts, you double-minded.

—James 4:7-8

↪ Give practical examples of what it means to resist the devil.

↪ Give examples of what it means to draw near to God.

A child who learns how to overcome unpleasant situations and genuine problems lives confidently, boldly, and with inner strength, courage, peace, and joy. Such a child may be temporarily fearful but need never give in to fear. What a wonderful legacy to leave your children!

> Exhort bondservants to be obedient to their own masters, to be well pleasing in all things, not answering back, not pilfering, but showing all good fidelity, that they may adorn the doctrine of God our Savior in all things.
>
> —Titus 2:9-10

๛ Put the following principles into your own words:

Be obedient:

Be well pleasing:

Don't answer back:

Don't pilfer:

Show good fidelity:

How can these principles apply in your job or other daily responsibilities?

Chasten your son while there is hope, And do not set your heart on his destruction.

—Proverbs 19:18

When is the time of "hope" in a child's life, in terms of discipline?

This verse implies that a lack of discipline in a child's early life will lead to his destruction. Why? What responsibility does this place upon a parent?

❧ Today and Tomorrow ❧

TODAY: I CAN OVERCOME SIN AND SATAN ONLY WHEN I'M WEARING THE ENTIRE ARMOR OF GOD.

TOMORROW: I WILL REMEMBER DAILY TO PUT ON GOD'S ARMOR, AND I WILL TEACH MY CHILDREN TO DO THE SAME.

❧ Notes and Prayer Requests: ❧

Lesson 10

In Position to Receive God's Rewards

---------------- ✎ **In This Lesson** ✎ ----------------

LEARNING: WHERE DO WE DRAW THE LINES BETWEEN WORKING HARD AND
GIVING GENEROUSLY?

GROWING: HOW CAN I TRAIN MY CHILD TO RECEIVE GOD'S BLESSINGS AND
REWARDS?

Every parent wants his child to be successful in life. But what does that means in terms of leaving a legacy? From the Bible standpoint, it means training your child to be a good steward of all his resources—first and foremost, his *life*—and to be a generous giver to God's work and to those in need. Good stewardship and generosity are the keys that unlock God's storehouse of blessing.

Good Stewardship

As a foundation for good stewardship, we are wise to teach our children to have a right attitude about money, the use of material possessions, and the relationship between faith and work.

Our attitude toward money must be free of envy, greed, and idolatry.

People make things into idols. They live to acquire things; they base their self-esteem upon the possession of material goods—from wearing the "right" labels to driving the "right" kind of car; they routinely compare their possessions to those of others, and they are habitually unhappy with what they have and desire more. Teach your child that God comes first—always! Jesus taught in Matthew 6:33:

> But seek first the kingdom of God and His righteousness, and
> all these things shall be added to you.

Our emphasis in life is to be on the pursuit of those things that are eternal, not on things that rust, wear out, or rot away (see Matthew 6:20–21).

> Therefore put to death your members which are on the earth:
> fornication, uncleanness, passion, evil desire, and covetous-
> ness, which is idolatry.
>
> —Colossians 3:5

Why does Paul say that covetousness (or materialism) is idolatry? Why is materialism listed alongside of fornication and other "really bad sins"?

⟳ What does it mean to "put to death your members"? What sort of "death" is involved in overcoming materialism?

Our position toward money should be neutral—it is what we do with money that counts.

Money and material possessions in themselves are neither good nor bad. God is far more concerned about our attitudes toward money than He is about our current bank statements. Are we trusting in our riches for security? Are we hoarding possessions in fear of being without sufficient supply? Are we holding back from doing good with our money? Are we so consumed with the idea of making money and buying things that we ignore our relationship with God? These are attitudes that God wants us to overcome.

To a great extent, a child adopts the attitude of his parents toward money and material possessions. Reflect upon your own attitude toward money and material goods. Your attitude is the attitude that your child will mimic.

But they lie in wait for their own blood, They lurk secretly for their own lives. So are the ways of everyone who is greedy for gain; It takes away the life of its owners.

—Proverbs 1:18-19

✐ Explain in your own words how being greedy for gain is like plotting against your own life.

✐ What is your own attitude toward material possessions? What attitude are you seeing reflected in your children's lives?

We are commanded to work honestly.

The Bible clearly states that able-bodied people are to work and provide for their own needs. It speaks very strongly against procrastination, laziness, and a lack of diligence. We are wise to teach our children how to work and to value work. Children should be given various responsibilities and chores around the house and, at appropriate times, should be encouraged to earn part of their spending money. Reward your child for jobs well done with praise and words of appreciation. Require your child to work honestly and with integrity.

> ...If anyone will not work, neither shall he eat. For we hear that there are some who walk among you in a disorderly manner, not working at all, but are busybodies. Now those who are such we command and exhort through our Lord Jesus Christ that they work in quietness and eat their own bread.
>
> —2 Thessalonians 3:10-12

What is the connection between not working and being a busybody?

What is your child's attitude toward work? How much does this reflect your own attitude?

We are commanded to trust God to provide what we need and to guide our work.

Teach your child to give his best effort to honest work, and then to trust God to provide ample reward for his work. Help your child discover the work that is best suited to his natural God-given talents and abilities, and to become trained and skilled in that area of work. Pray with your child that God will give him wisdom, strength, and enthusiasm for work and that he will be able to maintain a high level of quality in all that he undertakes.

What are your emotional responses to these words:

Work:

Prosperity:

Greed:

Wealth gained by dishonesty will be diminished, But he who gathers by labor will increase.

—Proverbs 13:11

Where is the balance between trusting God to provide for our needs, and being responsible to earn a living?

Generosity in Giving

Make giving a part of your child's training from his earliest days. Teach your child to be obedient in giving to God's work, and encourage him to be *generous* toward others who are in need. The Bible teaches, "God loves a cheerful giver" (2 Corinthians 9:7). Those who give generously will receive generously. This does not mean that a person should give himself into debt. Nor should our giving ever be done to gain the approval of others. Our giving is to be like our work and our obedience: *as to the Lord.*

Make sure that your child has something to put into the offering plate each Sunday when he goes to church. If he is receiving an allowance or payment for work, encourage him to give a tithe (one-tenth) to the Lord. One of the clearest passages in the Bible about giving is in Malachi 3:8–12, and what a promise is included in that passage for those who tithe faithfully!

> "Will a man rob God? Yet you have robbed Me! But you say, 'In what way have we robbed You?' In tithes and offerings. You are cursed with a curse, For you have robbed Me, Even this whole nation.

> "Bring all the tithes into the storehouse, That there may be food in My house, And prove Me now in this," Says the LORD of hosts, "If I will not open for you the windows of heaven And pour out for you such blessing That there will not be room enough to receive it.

> "And I will rebuke the devourer for your sakes, So that he will not destroy the fruit of your ground, Nor shall the vine fail to bear fruit for you in the field," Says the LORD of hosts; "And all nations will call you blessed, For you will be a delightful land," Says the LORD of hosts.

God expects every person to tithe—the tithe is given to God *from* our increase and *for* our increase. It is the way that we open the door of our finances both to give and to receive God's blessing. It is an act of faith that we are trusting God to grow the "seed" that we plant and to cause it to multiply on our behalf. The child who learns to give generously to the Lord's work and to others becomes unselfish. Such a child is going to receive great blessings—not only from God, but from other people.

✍ What does the Malachi passage above teach about tithing regularly?

...He who sows sparingly will also reap sparingly, and he who sows bountifully will also reap bountifully.

—2 Corinthians 9:6

✍ Explain how being generous is similar to sowing and reaping crops.

Jesus taught very specific things about our giving. These are key principles to teach your children:

    ∾ We are to give to the needy, wherever we find them (Matthew 25:37–40).

    ∾ We are to give sacrificially (Mark 12:41–44).

    ∾ We are to give without a great public display or show (Matthew 6:1–4).

    ∾ It is more blessed to give than to receive (Acts 20:35).

The tithe is the standard for giving to God's work, yet we must always recognize the truth of 1 Chronicles 29:14: "All things come from You, and of Your own we have given You." Everything that we have and are is a gift of God to us, and *all* of what we are and have belongs to God for His use at *all* times.

A child who is trained to be a generous giver and a good steward of all that he has been given from God—his time, his talents, his resources, his energy—is going to live in sufficiency and in *satisfaction and fulfillment*. What a wonderful legacy it is for a child to be taught *how* to give and receive from God!

So let each one give as he purposes in his heart, not grudgingly or of necessity; for God loves a cheerful giver. And God is able to make all grace abound toward you, that you, always having all sufficiency in all things, may have an abundance for every good work.

—2 Corinthians 9:7-8

_⊚ According to these verses, what is the most important aspect of tithing? How can a person gain this?

_⊚ According to these verses, for what purpose does God bless us when we tithe cheerfully?

Your Children Follow in Your Footsteps

As we have noted repeatedly in this study, your children follow in *your* footsteps. A pastor, teacher, or other adult may be influential in a child's life, but nobody can leave a legacy to a child in the same way that you can as a parent. Ask the Lord to help you today to leave to your child the legacy that *He* wants you to leave.

No parent is a perfect parent—such a person has never existed and never will exist. Every parent has faults and failures. What we must do as parents is to trust God to help us, to guide us, and to do for our child what we are incapable of doing. We are to trust God to work all things together for the good of our child (Romans 8:28). Desire today to be the best parent that you can possibly be and to leave the greatest spiritual legacy that you can possibly leave to your child. And then give your efforts to the Lord and trust Him to use your example and your teaching in whatever ways He desires to bring about the perfection and completion of your child. God's ultimate goal is to see your child grow to maturity in the likeness of Jesus Christ. Make that your goal, too!

> The hand of the diligent will rule, But the lazy man will be put to forced labor.
>
> —Proverbs 12:24

⌖ Who do you know who has risen to success through hard work? Who has been forced into menial tasks because of laziness?

What exactly is diligence? How can you teach that quality to your children?

Today and Tomorrow

TODAY: WE ARE CALLED TO BE BOTH DILIGENT AND GENEROUS.

TOMORROW: I WILL WORK TO BE A MODEL OF DILIGENCE AND GENEROSITY THAT MY CHILDREN CAN IMITATE.

Notes and Prayer Requests:

☙ Notes and Prayer Requests: ☙